The Muses Will Love You Dearly

The Muses Will Love You Dearly

Fait Muedini

K&B

Published by
Kennedy & Boyd
an imprint of
Zeticula Ltd
Unit 13
196 Rose Street
Edinburgh
EH2 4AT
Scotland

http://www.kennedyandboyd.co.uk
admin@kennedyandboyd.co.uk

Text Copyright © Fait Muedini 2022
Cover image:
Joseph Paelinck (1781-1839), *The Dance of the Muses*

First published in this format 2022

ISBN 978-1-84921-134-5 paperback

To Kaltrina

Acknowledgements

I am grateful to my wife Kaltrina for her continued support and encouragement throughout the writing of these poems.
Thank you to my children Edon and Dua Muedini for being their wonderful selves.
Thank you as well to my parents Atli and Mudzefer Muedini.
Lastly, I want to thank Stuart Johnston at Kennedy & Boyd for his belief in my work, and comments during the publishing of the book.

Thank you as well to all those who have read my poetry.

Contents

May the Muses Accept Our Offerings

The eve before
  a lifetime in the making.

  Prior generations' sacrifices
culminate in today's creative potential.

Free the mind from thieves with their hands out
  in your pocket, in your hopes, in your fantasies
slashing tires
  and locking you in an open room, with golden
handcuffs, but
      no notebooks.

Pens stocked and loaded
  Endless possibilities.
Withhold self-criticism
  and curb expectations.
Life was not meant to be ordered,
  and now,
      for a short time, it is not.
  All idols.

This evening, we rebel for our unstructured space to create.
  Not unlike the supplication before the first day of
fasting

      we call to the muses to accept our offerings.

Show Up

I'm here
Imploring you
In the middle of the night
Like a wolf
Howling at the moon
Supplicating to a dark sky

Show up.

I've done all you ask. I've sat at my desk
Day after day, after day
Staring at lived space.

I've walked through airports
And wandered bazaars and bookstores
                    on the off chance
That you arrive.

I don't care how or where you enter.

Just grant me words.

Just pay a visit.

The Muses Will Start Running

Create an inviting atmosphere.
      A home surrounded with luscious lighting
           and lingering aromas.
                  Candles and incense shall do.
Play the music of the muses,
      whatever that may be.
Now, finding the right song might take some effort shuffling
through records
           or online playlists.
But when the correct piano keys are struck,
      or when the unparalleled horn is heard,
                the muses will start running.

Our lives are merely meant to anticipate
      and react to
their arrival.

Of A Man Renewed

A bodyguard with unlimited bullets.

        Protect the muses
                at any and all cost.

Fight against those who
take shots at the spark
of creativity.

Builds moats around the castle
Snipers and cannons
To protect the canon
Which pours from the essence
Of a man renewed.

Falling Out of Pockets

I awoke to loud sounds
      in the still so early morning,
There,
      muses.
               Arms stretched into the sky
somewhat like whirling dervishes,
      all,
          together,
moving marvelously.

Quickly,
      let's grab a large cloth
and run around
          underneath and in between
collecting gold dust and diamonds
      falling out of the pockets
              of those who dance.

Arms Heavy with Poems

Early arrival,
but no rewards just yet.

Let's just hope the muses
appreciate the commitment
and visit from Mt. Olympus,
        or wherever else they or their offspring might now
reside,
arms heavy with poems.

The Giant Within You

Caught in a shell of himself,
      regret, upon regret, upon regret.

Amplified lilies sing synchronously.

Winds whipping,

while dreams disintegrate
      one mundane day at a time.

The canvas sits as
      a reminder of the careless creative,
            who took chances,
and was chained to nothing.

In this pool
      we wish to swim.

Elevate the enlightened ambitions
      and destroy all other evidence from the scene.

The crime?

Attempted murder.
      Someone tried to demolish the designer.

The muses shall not stand for such a thing.

Hard at work plucking harp strings,
      echoing vocals,
            and playing dangerously,
frantically,
      in hopes of awakening
            the giant within you.

Blood From the Hearts of Muses

All we do is fill the pen
      with blood from the hearts of those who inspire.

        They,
           happy to sacrifice themselves for a
        cause so extraordinary.

This is the life of the muse.

Privy to the eyes of Earth,
They joyfully rid themselves

           of any lingering ego.

"In your art, we exist."
"In everything else, we die."

Become Beholden to Beautiful Breathing

A mind full of files to be read
        by the muse
                whose mission it is
to sift through the piles and piles of
        pages,
saying,

"throw this out, throw that out."

"Here, take this instead."

Nourishment in the form of
        fresh logs for a fire.

Consume into a combustible flame
        everything that is extra, dull, and dead.

The muse is here for an ecstatic exorcism.

        Walk the jinn down to the gateway of the graves.
Let them lie there,
        abandoned in their insignificance.

Free from the
        obambulate with the intent of
                collecting fresh memories
                        to input into whatever words makes the
muses smile.
They saved your life, so now
        in turn,
                become beholden to beautiful breathing.

An affidavit of a life
        devoted to art.

Perpetual Poetry Pouring Profusely

Muses merry go round

Where they cease,
Only a dead poet knows.

Perpetual poetry
Pouring
Profusely.

Pages,
        steeped in the sweet sweat
of the playful goddesses.

Perceptions of Clarity

Hand on the Quran,
    Friday night,
        self-exiled
            inside a hallowed room, deserted,
with expectations that muses drop perceptions of clarity
    upon perforated parchment paper.

Ruzbihan danced with God until early dawn
    and afterwards, returned to somber sensibilities.

An out of body experience in the form of poetic annotations.

Thus Spoke the Muses

Lounge on cafes across the continent
       or meditate while walking in winter wilderness.

Worry not,
       for we are everywhere.

Do not allow a lack of imagination to
       impede progress of vocalization.

We never let an artist down.
       Ever.
All we require is a commitment.

Allah said: "take one step towards me, I'll take ten steps towards you.
       Walk towards me, I'll run towards you."

Thus spoke the muses.

Become Indispensable to the Muses

Become indispensable to the muses.

See, they need you,
like you need them.

The artist:
    full of capacities to create
        but able to do little of their own accord.

The muses:
    masters at motivating
        but useless when it comes to
            constructing art themselves.

Therefore,
    cultivate this partnership
carefully.

Write so many exalted words
    that the muses
        would deem life meaningless
could they not speak through your soul.

Searching for Treasures

I keep searching for treasures
    in nightmares that still haunt me
        years after their first surfacing.

I hunt for harnessed energy in torrential rainstorms
    the same winds
        that threw roof shingles around like
    frisbees,
    without reverence,
    without care.

Beauty resides in the crevices of the heart
    never meant to be opened or
    exposed to daylight.

I'll take the stress,
    all of it,
  if,
and only if
    somewhere,
    hidden, or out in the open,

    sits a muse
sharing secrets with me.

Let the revelations offered
        be buried under boulders
                    untouched in decades.

I don't care.
        Hungry for an inspiring internal journey,
                wrestling to articulate,
                        a writer accepts any costs that come
with the tradeoff of being associated with
        the muses.
In life, make sure to do business with an artist.
        They will likely trade the farm
                for a moment of
                            uninhibited
                    innovation.

Jump-Start

Now, this is the visit needed.
   Muses disguised as sounds
     playing through quiet
       or loudspeakers.
A jolt of lightening:
   a release of artistic possibilities.

Quick,
   take out the drum machine,
     set up the microphone,
and hit record.

We are capturing a moment here.

A car with a dead battery needs a jump-start
   to then proceed traveling cross country
     during a snowstorm,
       carrying an artist whose goal is to
stop at each sight
   and denote beauty through the brushstroke.

The Faucets of Creativity

Adherents begin arduous journeys
      to the Kaaba
           or Delphi
                 for any and all healing
                     from those divine sites.

But yet,
      we become conservative with resources
          pertaining to sustaining the muses?

Our prize into the annals of artists elevated
      is to spend every dime

for those that control
                  the faucets of
          creativity.

Calliope

It's funny how poets can waste a day filled with nothing,

    then they write one or two stunning sonnets,

        and feel as if they reached high productivity,
            conquering the world with their
  compositions.

We know the lies.

Consider yourself fortunate that Calliope not only visited,
        but also left you all the credit,
          so that the world would be none the
wiser.

Addicted to the Poetry

The muse proposes a few verses
    and sets them all out on the table.

Verbs, adjectives, and sharp rhythmic patterns.
    Somewhere, sometime,
        to be scrambled and organized.

An addict
    becomes intensely desperate
        to make a magical moment
            out of small letter particles.

A Harnessed High of Expressiveness

Have you ever had an argument with the muses?
      Guardians who withheld the inspiration
            that you indisputably needed to live?
This is where the alcohol comes in handy.

I've seen artists empty handed,
      on both knees
          begging out in an open public
             for small crumbs of ingenuity.
Anything to satiate the craving.

They do wild things, these writers. They talk to trees, stare at
clouds, and walk right into ditches.
      They search high and low for
          the jewels hidden in plain sight.

Speak to someone who has writer's block,
      watching the time tick
          with absolutely nothing to show for.

Desperation takes over,
      and that's when you learn
         exactly what an artist will do
             for a few harnessed
         highs of expressiveness.

The Path to Productivity

Moody and unforgiving.
        Relentless in the need to be
                the center of study.

Celebrity status
        with celebrity benefits.
Muses have the power to move moons,
        and so,
                when they please,
can easily help
        craft stories and construct characters.

For you, the peak of a profession.
        For them, just another Thursday.

This is the power of who you are dealing with.

        So, tread lightly, and offer appreciation after
appreciation
                after appreciation.

There are a thousand paparazzi
        each looking to take that million-dollar photo
                that will just as easily change their life, as it
would yours.

        You can be quickly forgotten.

Remember that when greeting those who galvanize,
        those who hold the power to shake your world
                into a state of submission.

The path to productivity
        depends on the sage who knows the way up the
convoluted mountainside.

Salutations of Indebtedness

Straight staring into the soul.
    A sample of what is yet to come.

Muses manifest the powers of creation, in absolute terms.
    What we have at our disposal is everything
        witnessed through the eyes of those that live to
inspire.
The looks were meant for madness
    to stir up the savant nature of the self.
An artist's abstraction realized.

We sing hymns in praise
    of those who prance around sprinkling stardust onto
canvases
        and into notebooks.
Salutations of indebtedness.

    A recognition of the impossibility of flying
        if not without the wings of those who wander
with the wind
        providing gifts to those in absentia.

Scintillating Visions of Seductiveness

A million muses with the grace
               to cause earthquakes to canvases,
      to leave artists with broken hearts,
               and revelations unlikely to be replicated.

Scintillating visions of seductiveness.

'Tis not to be.

      Clamoring minds,
               constructing laundry lists of chores
Each more constraining than the other
      of time, of self, of freedom.

Saying 'hello' used to be break the ice between future
collaborators
      destined to collide with conviction.
But no longer.
      Now, the world works from one destination to the next.

These muses have been given a scroll of errands

      each ever more erroneous to happiness than the other.
Death by a thousand thoughtless, unimaginative tasks.

A factory of training
      since birth
               until death.

With One Glance

A single asteroid can smash into the Earth,
        altering your core,
                and changing your entire trajectory.

Painters seek the smiling muse.
        Nourish with compliments,
                and forego all sanity.

You are dealing with an entity
        who has the power to erase a lifetime of errors
           with one glance.
                With one glance.

Authentic Muses

With time,
>the muses change.
A rotation of motivation.

But here's the beauty.
>Authentic muses hang not onto past glories,
or some currency of current relevancy.

>Even if never called upon again,
for the rest of eternity
they understand that,
>at some point,
>>it was they who incited a poem that echoes out
in the universe

>>forever.
Their resume needs nothing more.

No sulking here.

The finality of inspiration is well understood
>by those who comprehend
>>the specific purpose
>>>of their presence.

The Outcome of Inventiveness

Do muses get jealous?

    The answer is a resounding no,
        at least not the ones who lay down their life for
the art.

See, what most do not understand is that muses are
    selfless.
They give everything for a painting, a poem, and well-crafted
coat, a fadeaway jumper,
    or a synchronized swim routine.

The beloved doesn't care what causes their lover to beam.
    The happiness is the ultimate destination.

So, soak in scenes of inspiration.

We exist to express, and what is birthed is beloved and free.

Here are the signs of the passionate and pure hearted.

    The outcome of inventiveness.

Pinnacle

Bestow upon the bride layers and layers
    of laced gold,
        for a moment marked,
            a pinnacle in adulthood.
The muses watch proudly,
        finally observing the culmination of an intensity
unlike no other.
Sometimes, a punctuation point is needed to celebrate a job well
done,
    a life complete.

See, this is what art is. Art is a composite of all circumstances
    each choosing to appear in certain contexts,
        depending on the time, depending on the year,
        depending on the mood.

The muses carry emotions with them
        and, when summoned
deliver.
    The canvas becomes whole when all feelings finally
    coalesce.

Each Encounter

An accumulation of experiences
    are the cornerstones of poetry,
        of song,
Why?

Muses like to show off
    in a multitude of avatars
and manifestations.

Therefore,
    treat each encounter as an avenue for
        the muse to enter your heart
            into your consciousness,
                and onto your canvas.

Worth the Price of the Pain

High glare and glistening goals.

    A satisfaction unreachable,

unless, of course,
        the words flow at the price of
                everything else.

Only then shall the winds take your poems to distant lands
        to dusty corridors
            in libraries
                not visible by map
by only by heart.

The muses know the way.

    "Quickly, follow us."

Drop the entirety of burden
        and become calm in the company of the
            act of creation.

Camus told the story of Jonas:
        The man whom no one understood.
        The man who died for his art.

While the world may fail to comprehend,

        those who paved the path
            did so with syllables of gold.
Rest assured,
        while the road is one that few traverse,
            all sacrifices
                    are well worth
                    the price
of the pain.

Beauty Like No Other

Muses seen before,
       somewhere.

But certainly here,
          now.

They won't provide the insight easily.
       What is required is fixation, infatuation.

Then, maybe,
     just maybe,
         after extensive petitioning,
     in their jacket they reach,
finally providing but a few words.

What the artist sacrificed the world for:

     Beauty like no other.

Begging

We are beggars,
        completely at the mercy of the muses.

So, sit near the street
        risking being struct near the intersection,
                for an intercession,
a few scraps of food,
        some short sentences,
                since this may be all the almsgiving
                        for the evening.

Bow your head in gratitude.
        and on no account should you
                curse the skies for what has not been provided.

The artist accepts all offerings
        with open hands
                and an open heart.

Tomorrow shall be a new day.

When the Muses are Fed

How interesting
Sometimes they demand
Walks or meditation,
Sometimes innovative,
        unheard music,
And sometimes,
        the entire sun
                    throwing rays onto beaches,
                        palm trees and wide-mouthed
            oceans.
Give them what they wish for,
        because,
all is well,
        when the muses are fed.

The Muses Will Love You Dearly

The amount of love permeating through the pen
                                    will depend on the
                            following:

        What was your benefaction to the muses? Did you clear
the coffers?
                    Wash the baseboards, and prepare the guest
room?

        Imagination relies on nothing short of everything.

                            A million dream-killers haunting towns
across the globe.
        Don't become a victim to vanity, all for the price of
pretension and prestige.

                Follow the signposts.

In exchange for such loyalty?
                            More than the night will
                    provide.

The muses will love you dearly.

        But the moment of distraction is their cue to depart.

Stress-Test

Never let a muse catch you
    without a notebook,
        without a pen.

They love to flood weak damns
    with wonderful words
        just waiting for poets to be ill-prepared.

Muses love to stress-test,
    so that they can see
        who is here standing faithful to their voice.

The Muses Become Bored

Large cappuccinos get cold
      after fifty minutes or so.

Just about the time it takes
      for the muses to become bored.

This is how long you have to compose.

Muses Who Deliver Under Misery

Some muses are tied to misery.
　　　Melpomene stands at the forefront of tragedy.

But know that the ones who look for pain carry gold in their
palms
　　　and are sympathetic only to beings beaten by the
brutality of life.
　　　　　　Having traversed the road with rage,
Sadness
　　　Sadness
　　　　　Sadness.

Have you suffered deaths on your doorstep?
　　　These are the exact artists that select muses
　　　　　　　　　select.

In your torture,
　　　top-shelf art.

Smile and see how quickly these muses skirt away.

Cry deep, uncontrollable tears
　　　over everything that the world has stolen from you.

 Like a rainbow post rainfall,
　　　these muses knock on your closed door
　　　　　delivering a package of poems that will
　　　　　　　leave critics calling for your coronation
stating that only a possessed king could write such majestic
madness.

Offerings

A cacophony of similarities
    dressed up and disheveled.
Words
    still, the same,
        merely repeated and rehashed.

No, we need something stronger.

    The writer seeks sentences set to bring about breathes
of bewilderment,
        an awe-inspiring reaction that leaves the reader
            hollowed out and holy.

For the elixir, we must visit the muses.

Gold gilded gowns as offerings
    and a supplication where we admit
a penance for procrastination.
Our preclusive productivity
    lay only at our feet.

But please, overlook our errors.
    Absolve us of our aptness for distraction.

Heads are bowed in a humble state.
    Poor peasants pleading for charity.

What we request, respectfully,
    are potent poems
        so present
            so passionate
                that nature itself will have no
                choice but to stop and take
                notice.
These are but the simple longlists of those who craft verse.

All Ecstatic Expressions

The muses need not lavish dinners
        nor expensive coffee (although this helps).

They seek no special scenery

All they require is a soft spot to land
To spread their wings out freely,
And to speak special sounds.

Just keep a pen ready to record
                        all ecstatic expressions.

To Do Marvelous Things

Truncated and disheveled
   disease ridden and desolate
struck with an anxiety unbeknownst
   and a heartache ever endured

The muses know that
   your career is that their disposal.
With one look away,
     all prospects are pronounced dead on arrival.
So,
   treat them with extra attentiveness
     shower the grail granters with chests filled with
treasures
       and ironically, with the money made by
work prosaic.

The smirks on the faces--
   beauties who understand that they have the capabilities
to sign either
     the birth or death certificate of an artist.

So you plead, and you plead, and you plead...

Show up and shovel snow in February.
   One never knows when a muse, dressed in a long-tailed
dress
     decides to stroll up to your quarters, park
herself next to your writing hand
and emboldens you to do marvelous things.

If You Stay

There is always an option
                     to extend one's trip.

Muses shall never put you on the clock.

Routine is both a mark of commitment,
         but also, rigidity.

Remember that,
         and be content breaking continuity.

Often, it's the muses themselves
         that captivate you with the promise of something
special.

If you stay.

They Act Like This for You

Here,
    the muses are magical.
They hang from chandeliers
    spill liquor
        and throw plates against the parquet.
This is the show we came for.
    But stop watching
        and start writing.
They act like this for you.

Renewed Vows

A poet renews vows
        to stay committed to the craft.

Then, the muses
        already content with the output
Will do what they can
To ensure elegant examinations
Regarding the grander scale of life
Keep flowing.

The Silent Treatment

Today,
      I let the muses down.

They waited patiently by the door,
      sitting with stunning sentences,

But I walked right along,
      as if not recognizing their existence.

Still,
      I know where they can be found,
           nature trails, quiet lakes, or even the secluded
office.

Instead,
      I embarked upon a day of shopping,
         stopping only to treat myself to lunch.

But now,
      their revenge.

I, here, waiting for conversation,
      expecting some sort of utterance
         but being given
the silent treatment.

The Note

Waking up to see pages and pages
        from books
                          he himself wrote
scat
        ter
            ed

about the apartment,
        almost as if a thief came to look for something
hidden,
        and threw about papers
            to find what was being hunted.

But,
        in this case,
            this was not the case.

See,
here,
        in this instance,
            everything was spread about
        in quite a respectful way.
Furthermore,
        each work
            contained markings,
                highlights,
underlining,
        and exclamation points, in black, blue, and red inks,

as if,
        whoever did this
            was fully immersed,
                and equally enamored with
                    these sublime words.

Upon further examination of the room,

nearby,
        a short, poignant note was found,
                which, written in a careful calligraphy,
read:

                This used to be you.
                Return to yourself

Muses can sense washed up writers
        and they find dramatic,
                in your face
                        never to forget
        ways

of making their pleas
        for you to return
                        to a level
                                that once was
quite well known.

He Swears to the Muses

He swears to the muses
that interest in the vices
of the demon-filled city are gone.

A plea
        on both bended knees
for them to return.

Public self-admonishment
        self-immolation
if need be.

All this for some inspiration
into a pen
that if dry
may be what is used
to
strike straight into the neck.

"We are closer to him than his jugular vein"

Only so many second changes
until the meaning of "second" is so diluted
that the muses
have lost all interest
and murmured to each other,
"let us move on, for there are no writers who live here."

When Muses Strike to Kill

With hollowed out harpoons,
    and protruding veins
verifying anger
      the muses come and knock on your door at dusk.
The demand? A day's work of writing.

Most paintings picture muses smiling
    and dancing to song.

The truth is often anything but.

      Sure, when artists act like artists,
          parties continue for countless hours.

This,
      this is akin to a wedding ceremony
         where works of wonder meet God.

But when shirking of responsibility to create
    is now the norm,
        where those who were birthed to bequeath
    exquisite expressions
          have failed to follow through,

well, that's when the muses strike to kill.

The Graves of Muses Who Lost Hope

Underestimated walks
around hallowed halls towards a
crying cemetery.

The tombstones of muses who pushed too hard
for whom they vouched for.

All they wanted
        was for you to just pick up
                        a pencil
and write.

The Lord scolded them to give up their belief, since the artist
they backed
        is of no use.

Not a sonnet scribbled,
        the corpse sits idly,
                alive but dead.

And because of this,
        the muses stopped breathing.
The pain was just too much.

Muses live on the fumes of creativity.

Sunshine is the light that sparks
        when the ballpoint prances on the page.

And you,
        you killed her.

How selfish, how lazy, how unjust.

A cheerleader in your corner.
A saint begging with a rice bowl.
Asking for something,
anything to nourish her dying spirit.

Yet,
you couldn't muster a minute
to guide your fingers over a few guitar strings.

And now she's gone.

In the central courtyard
are the graves of the muses
who lost hope.

The Letter

Deadbeat artists are the absolute worst.

The obligation to the creative process is real,
and shirking on such responsibilities is as low as one
gets.

The talent is there, so use it.
Instead, you would rather get drunk at some low-lit bar
using the vocation of artist in vain,
to score some praise, and maybe a free
drink or two.

You come from a long lineage of greats.
They who poured their fears onto paper,
who lit up the stage with sound,
who expressed manifestations of
perfection, perfectly.

We know you need help. For so long, we have tried to guide you
back onto
the path of promise.

We have called repeatedly,
asking for some attention,
for a commitment to what counts.

But nothing. Dead silence,
  all the while, watching you go about
    with a pompousness of a swindler,
      who has gotten away with too many
thefts
and
  somehow
    thinking s/he conquered the world.

But we know better.
  We know what can be achieved
    with your talent

  with your life.
Please come back,
  before it's too late.

Signed,

The Muses

The Maddened Muse

A muse gone mad
        haunting the very grounds
                where she was married off
to a beloved who promised her
        a life brimming with poetry and paintings.

In the beginning,
        words flowed
                and music marveled.
Love filled the studio
        as the mind consecrated the beautiful.
A birth bestowed.

But,
        at some point,
                a complacency crept in,

lingered,
and eventually
        led to a murder.

The days became months, and then, became years.
        All the while,
                she waited patiently,
pleading for purpose
        and a restoration of passion.

But nothing became,
        until, one fateful night,
                sharp knives plunged
                        until the antique rug was
drenched with nothing but a shell of a self.

Without any evidence of a physical altercation,
    he killed her spirit
        with his indifference to life.

Little did he predict, that on that very same evening,
    the dead took the dead.

The muse bemoans the miscreant
    who broke the only law of matter:
        An artist is born only to create.

Ghostly and ghastly,
    now nightly,
        the deceased muse wanders the hallways

        Bellowing out:

"Beware of False Artists. Beware of False Artists. Beware of
False Artists."

In those words lay a covenant broken,
        a bond obliterated by the one who sulks in
sluggishness,
        who lingers in lethargy,
          who has spoiled the fruits of
talent,
        sunset, after sunset,
after sunset.

A muse's life
    destroyed.

Most Sad of All

So, you wanted ideal conditions to write?
    Here, here is what we offer.

Despise winter blues? We pushed the calendar forward.
    Spring is now sprouting its head above ground.

Feeling restricted by time?
    We have set aside some days where,
        not so miraculously
            hours have been harvested
                for the culmination of
        creativity.

What else do you need?
    Please, tell us.

We are a boss who gives you a blank check,
    work-from-home flexibility
        and little accountability,
            and only insist
on authentic output.

If this is not enough,
    then maybe you don't have the dedication to be an
artist.

We know you harbor the talent
                    to be quite special,
which makes this entire situation
    all the more sad.

Bedridden

The muse,
      bedridden,
            and out of breath.

Anxious and annoyed
      and emotions stirred,
            all at once.

And by whom?

The artist,
      who would rather collect pieces of paper
and sit idly
      day after day after day,
            instead of embracing the emotions of life,
and birth whatever may result
      out of such love making.

Unwritten Words

The muses hate lingering
       unwritten words.

"I'll just jot it down in the morning," you utter.

It's as if a world class pastry chef
baked a delicious cake
covered with fine toppings
and stuffed with rich flavorful jams
and you push the plate away,
saying,
       rather arrogantly,
              that you will have a bite tomorrow.

Show disrespect like that,
       and shame on you for expecting any gifts
           ever again.

Let the waiter carry the cake to someone who is much more
appreciative.

You Will Be Dead to Them

The mind is a rambunctious child
    reliant on Rx
        to become calm.
Blissfulness is besieged by a bevy of beings
    each set on pressing an agenda of insignificance.

Quiet contemplation cannot succeed without
    some sort of protection money
        to imposing kingpins
            who will only then take it upon
themselves
            to care.
Pay the cost.
    What are we talking about here?
        A rather small sum
            in exchange for a semblance of the
price of peace.

The fitness trainer will not walk into a kitchen
    where the pantry is filled with sugary sweets.

Muses are also particular.
    If they see a side-eye
        glancing to check email.
            they will shut down,
                and just like that,
you will be dead to them.

A Prisoner to a Life Undeserved and Undesired

Under no circumstances
    should you place
        a quota on creativity.

Do the muses look like they belong in some bureaucracy,
    bustling away for the sake of a monthly sales target?

Why, you would have a revolt of epic proportions.

Imagine telling a muse to concentrate on some spreadsheet
    for hours on end.

Good luck with that.

The muse would likely
    get up and aimlessly wander about
        without much concern for numbers,

            and even less for getting fired.

        Furthermore, can you imagine the pain you would cause
           If the Muse *had* to sit and stare at a screen
               with no poetic pronunciations?

It wouldn't surprise me if a few of them would begin
    crying uncontrollably
        right there in the open cubicle
distraught and dejected
    unable to look themselves in the mirror and smile.

A prisoner to a life undeserved and undesired.

Unfinished Manuscripts

What is it going to take?

Does the muse have to drag you by the ear,
        straight to your desk?

Must they make a scene at the grocery store
        throwing cereal boxes and breaking bottles

                                                across

different aisles
for admiration?

Will you not take heed?

Words
        languish in the waiting room.
A hospital housing
your body.
        Stale and motionless,
doctors
        frantically trying to shock you back to life.

Still, even if alive,
        how many hours
                                wasted
doing nothing?

Laziness makes the muses miserable.

Unfinished manuscripts pile upon each other.

Upon your death

The very same documents shall be used to kindle flames at the
funeral,
        of a person who could have been
                a magnificent writer.

A Muse's Lament

Where are you going?

Who else has your focus?

Am I not good enough for your words?

Does my appearance fail to foster your creative self?

What can I do differently?
                                        Let me try.

                                                I beg of you.

                Give me another chance to make ~~write~~ right
        what is wrong.

What do you want from me?

                        I'll give up my gowns of lavish.
                All opulent ornaments will be melted down
                        and sold off to fund your future.

                                Anything it takes,
                        as long as these actions
                                move you
                                        to write.

Yet, you turn your back?

How can you ignore me?
                I was there for your first cursive lines in
                        elementary school
                And by your beside when you
                        fought the flu while
                                working on those high school essays.

                        And college. The era where deep ideas
                        were first sparked.

Who lit that match?
                              It was me.

You, influenced by Unamuno, Sartre, Gibran, and Rumi?
                         Past protégés of mine.

               Yet, of all the creatives I've known
                         you are,
                                        by far
                    the least grateful.
          Unlike you, most were ecstatic with what I
     brought, and thanked me continuously in prose.

               And while others I encouraged were more
     temperamental,
     At least they sat down and finished their projects
                    completing their calling.
     But you,
                    your arrogance thinks it knows better.

               The cause of my death will be
                    that I picked the wrong horse.

     I could have visited a thousand other upstarts
               each thirsting to write novels, screenplays, or
                    sing songs that illuminate
                              the human condition.

     Instead, I spoke up and advocated for who I thought was
                    a unique artist inspired.

     And because of this ill-fated choice,
     What am I left with?
               Nothing.
                    All because you chose
                         the petty distractions
                              of an ever so material world,
                                   instead of me.

Blame Nothing on Them

Left to your own devices,
        most creatives will die
            drunk
                in debt and
                    filled with doubt.

Never having scribbled a sentence,

the muses are the loyal friends who
        nurse you with treatments
            to ensure a quick recovery.

They sing mantras
        and light candles
            throughout the nightly vigils
in hopes
        that your psyche will be summoned back to
                (a passionate) life.

Yet, you lay lifeless, with a pulse,
                producing nothing
      that
            embodies your emotions.
                The only thing you were
            meant to do.

So,
        blame your inabilities to create
            on confusion,
                on laziness
                  on willfully
                    knowingly
that you,
      yes you,
                wasted an abundance of talent.

But not on them. Blame nothing on them.

An Inauthentic Life

Muses staring into foggy mirrors
      looking for the prodigal son
            to step out of the demands of society
and live freely.

When they see you, they see an extension of themselves.
      Do not let the muses down.

Happiness arises when the parent witnesses the child
accomplish high feats
      with fervent love.
An inauthentic life is the highest form of disappointment.

The Temporal, Over Time, Takes Talent

The muses require obsession.
        A constant commitment to a craft.

The expectation is that the outside world will be shunned.
        Nothing less will suffice.

                They are here to remind you
                        that all distractions are death sentences.

We have but a finite period for which to weave fine silk into
        a robe fit for a prince.

The temporal, over time, takes talent.

You must get to work,
                and stay active
                        to save yourself
                                by becoming eternal.

Intercessors of an Artist Unarrived

If you could go back to before being born
        and watch the muses plead with God to
                grant upon you the capacities to create,
to write profound poetry,
        to arrange paint in patterns original,
                you would be engulfed in your own tears.

                Out of their gift of gratitude

these beings spent what seemed like an eternity
        at the feet of The Supreme
                hunched over humbly,
                        forehead to the floor,
interacting as agents,
                intercessors of an artist unarrived.

Knowing this, you would not once undervalue these saintly
seconds
        the sensations of stimulation
        the depth connected with diving into an artform that
                was destined for you,
                        you, and only you.

Anything Less is Sacrilege

How many more signs do you need
    to stay inside today
        and write?

The muses have painted the pavement with frost.
    A snowstorm meant to be weathered in shelter.

    And, for you,
        this means lounging about with your letters,
with your thoughts,
    and,
        soon,
            with words created and arranged
    in an astonishing fashion.
        Or, at least in astonishingly *true* fashion.

The muses care not for fame,
    shock value
        or even for paradigm altering poetry.

All they want is to see that you speak your "You."

    Anything more is pompous boasting
        and anything less is sacrilege.

Answer Only to the Muses

Answer only to the muses,
  for their voice is the only voice that matters.

  The true self
    flows through the witnessing of the goddesses.

Therefore,
  have tunnel vision from the outside world.

Why give any value to the opinions of billions
  who themselves are void of passion,
  and provide absolutely nothing positive for you?
Understand who feeds you,
  and never, ever waver.

Tonight

The triumph when the demons of decaying talent
        are conquered.

Tonight, we celebrate with free verse,
        with song,
                with patterned dance
and continuous
       gratuity
to the muses
        who have granted upon us the greatest honor
                by showing up to our banquet
                        with boxes of bread and bourbon.
For those who drink,
        drink.
For those who abstain,
        trays filled with sweet preserves--
                honeys and marmalade
encapsulated intoxication
        of many kinds.

Shelves filled with authors who were moved
        by one muse or another.

None of that matters.
        The dessert table is
                filled by our guests with enough gifts
                        to appease even the most clamorous
of composers.

        Tonight, we write.

Just Write

Invisible aspirations are muses pushing the limits of possible.

Roads need to be cleared
    boulders moved
        A path forward.

Muses labor tirelessly
    toiling
pouring concrete
    removing debris
        and any other excuse keeping you from being
            well, you.

So, show a little appreciation.
    They ask not for assistance, nor thanks.

Just write.

When an Artist Decides to Become an Artist

The trumpet lingers in isolation
as the quartet played their respective roles
        before
packing up for the evening.

What is meant to be heard
will be heard, so the muses assure.

A retrospective can only be housed
When an artist decides to become an artist.

Muses Love to Dance in Darkness

What needs to be done, needs to be done.
  Shirk not the joyous and blessed responsibilities of
family.
However, all other time must be guarded with your life.
Succumb to nothing.
  no fear
  no distortions
  no manipulation
      by colleagues
      by corporations
      by cynics.

Your time is your time.

  Submit to the creativity of one's own identity.
Wonder in the beauty of an artistic minefield.
  Ideas pronounce themselves after the muses have
awaken,
      with slightly frazzled hair
Long dresses of glamour
      midnight candle wax just dripping over
        symbolism of the poor man paying his due.
Now, this morning,
      showered with rewards of lyrics, or images, or musical
notes.
        Arm yourself with the appropriate medium to
  capture
        all that is conceived:

        Muses love to dance in darkness.

Mountain Fairies

The zanas
        linger upon mountains
                awaiting the aspiring artist
to make the arduous ascension,
        the same creative
                whose want is nothing but to whisper wishes to
        these muses.

Precious metals
        are not haphazardly handed out to the masses.

In no path of life
        should we reward quick results.

We must weed out the committed from the slightly serious.

Therefore, these elusive entities
        will put you through creative hell.

But remember: the recompense will be nothing short of
transcendent.

The Muses Share Sacred Syllables

I'm amazed at how
    the muses keep leaving poems
      for me to speak.

All writers will tell you: at any moment
We all but expect the words to wither
Leaving a barren shell of a tree.

But somehow, with God's grace
    the muses never get tired of pushing poets to write.

I wonder if these mythical entities sit together
    and speak to each other,
        shower him with more prose,
           more, more, more...
I believe
    that in their discussions
        with one another
        they said:
"Since he recalls us
Throughout the busied day
We shall in turn
Douse his demons with kerosine
Burning away impurities
So that all that remains
Are our sacred syllables."

The Rest Is Up to You

The muses have circled your abode since 4:00am
        waiting for the moment you awake.

Excited at what can develop,
        like a child awaiting a day filled with
                roller coasters and
                        water parks
They know what lies in store...

        potentially.

See, the rest is up to you.

An Army of Enforcers

You are the clues to which God created the universe,

the something which was made from nothing,
        something great,
                something that sparkles and is breathtaking
and complete
and we stay
        staring in awe.

This is what you offer.

        But to do this,
                to live atop mountains
                        having spilled every last drop of ink,
you will need an army of enforcers to protect you.

That's where the muses come in.

        Armed and dangerous,
                a defense unit for the golden child
who was placed on this planet to paint.

Do that
        and let them worry about everything else getting in your
way.

Protecting Their Poets

The muses will surprise you.

They always have a way of making you question the unfolding of
existence
        and how
        from a seemingly depleted
                inventory of words
arise a few more sentences
        equally vibrant,
        equally powerful.

For this reason, we happily spend savings, and youthful years
                        to these mythical martyrs
they who are willing to die their glorified death
        protecting their gods,
                protecting their poets.

The Space of Certainty

Live without lethargic tendencies.

The purpose is self-provided,
    self-propelled,
        self-sustained.
The avatars of an alternate actuality are stale and fragmented.
    For the only suitable self is the self that
        says no to
wild weeds that look to choke the fresh bed of flowers
    suffocating such beauty with the act of being.
We are here to witness The Real.
    Tell us what that might be.
    Even better.
Show us that version of ourselves.

Let the muses prevent any intruders from entering
the space of certainty.

Then and Only Then

So, are we here to dance?
　　　Well then,
　　　　　　let's dance.

An inability to encapsulate the suffering
　　　personified in personalities
　　　　　　spread across a ballroom floor.

Look at the poet,
　　　holding a notebook in his hand
　　　　　　racing to scribble whatever iterations of
truth
made their way into that room
　　　　　that night.

"You must say no to everything else"
　　　declared the muses,
　　　　　who shined the shoes and straightened the tie,
before sending the artist out into the night.

"We can hear all that corrupts your concentration, your
objectivity, your love."
　　　"Destroy anything that builds a nest in your heart."

Fireside chats are places of possibilities,
　　　and so are strolls through Indianapolis nights.
Divulge nothing.
　　　No disasters this evening.

Who spills ample wine onto oak flooring
　　　and lives to tell about it?
The poet, that's who.

Muses laugh most when encountering an original experience.
They have been given flowers.
What they need are more raw,
more poignant,
more suppressed sentiments.

When you start to cry at the realization that what arises from inside
is sufficient enough to lead a caravan of pilgrims
to weep tears
onto the road
of repentance,
then, and only then, have you found your voice.

Nothing More, Nothing Less

In the inexplicable universe
    muses laugh flowingly
        without an ounce of self-awareness.

In this country, all notions of past must be left at the gates
    where the gravediggers shall proceed
        to bury your body.
            A service free of charge.

In return, all that is asked is that
    you hold the present
        with extraordinary care
            and let your art capture this *now*.

Nothing more, nothing less.

Gaze Into Eyes Infatuated

Set for sound,
    but the microphone chord was cut
sharply and sternly
    with saffron dipped scissors
        upon first glimpse of your muse.

Butterflies argue over whose
coats dishevel the scholars.

    All gets ignored
        in hyperbaric chambers.

Plant poetry pamphlets
near sacred spaces,
shared spaces,
silent spaces.

Unspeakable majesty.

The mind creates a lived-out fantasy.

The heart picks up the first spear.
Straight to the depths of the sea.

Insatiable thirst
    and unquestionable love.

        Gaze into eyes infatuated.

Monster

Wide eyed and completely caffeinated
            absorbed in a medium
                        elusive to an outside world.
Between midnight and sunrise,
        here, right here,
                sits the composite of a creative, unleashed.
Words get spit out like hot fire
            burning down any and all buildings
                    standing in their way.

The muses sit with matches and laugh
        knowing that they have created a monster.

A Fulfilled Life

There is a saying
               that the professor teaches
                  the new,
                       soon to be cohort of muses
regarding how to select
        the artists that they choose to energize.

"Search for those who have a gleam in their eye
        and are willing give everything for their art."

A proper selection is the benchmark of a successful career as a
muse.

In the end,
        A muse will know whether their existence was spent
fruitfully,
               beaming with content,
                  or in vain,
        if,
when you view your poet, your painter, your tailor,
        can you say,
             about them,
                  unequivocally,

"What a Fulfilled Life!"

The Muses at your Deathbed

The muses shall visit you on your deathbed
      and cry.

Why?

Because,
      throughout your time here on Earth,
            you showed them respect and love
                fully conceived
                    fully displayed
in books,
in art,
in song.

And because of this,
      even here, during your very last moments,
          when frail, weak, and weary

listen closely,
      as you shall hear the muses whisper while weeping:

"One more poem. Just one more,"
      as they place the pen into your hand, grip your fingers
for you
        and guide your script sideways.

Dr. Fait Muedini is the Frances Shera Fessler Professor and Director of International Studies at Butler University in Indianapolis, Indiana. He has published several articles and books, including publications in outlets such as Foreign Affairs, Palgrave MacMillan, and Cambridge University Press. He is also the author of the poetry book *Idolatry of the Translated Forms*, published by Kennedy & Boyd.

www.ingramcontent.com/pod-product-compliance
Lightning Source LLC
Chambersburg PA
CBHW060055100426
42742CB00014B/2847